Notes from the Column of Memory

Also by Wendy Drexler

Before There Was Before
Buzz, Ruby, and Their City Chicks (co-author)
Western Motel
Drive-ins, Gas Stations, the Bright Motels (chapbook)

Notes from the Column of Memory

Wendy Drexler

Terrapin Books

© 2022 by Wendy Drexler
Printed in the United States of America.
All rights reserved.
No part of this book may be reproduced in any manner, except for brief quotations embodied in critical articles or reviews.

Terrapin Books
4 Midvale Avenue
West Caldwell, NJ 07006

www.terrapinbooks.com

ISBN: 978-1-947896-56-7
Library of Congress Control Number: 2022938430

First Edition

Cover art: Judith Greenwald
Begin, 2009
12" x 12" Combined media/encaustic on panel

Cover design: Diane Lockward

for Julia, Noah, Hannah, and Herb

Contents

One

Red-Eared Slider	7
Corral	8
My Father as a Taxidermied Fox	10
Groundhog	11
Oranges	12
Barbra Streisand Takes Her Two Cloned Dogs to Visit Their Mother	14
Hurled in the Grip	16
Hurling the Menhaden	18
Bluebird	19
Yellow Jacket	20
Notes from the Column of Memory: One	21

Two

Outbreak	25
Traffic Jam on the 405 North	26
The Only Softshell Turtle in Walden Pond	27
Apology to My Ovaries	28
To Prove That I Am Not a Robot	30
Five Knots and a Space	32
Eye of the Storm	34
Cézanne Still Life Painted by My Mother	36
Winter Ghazal	37
Coming Upon a Young Screech Owl	38
At Intermission	40
The Gannets at Cape St. Mary's, Newfoundland	42

Three

Burial of a Woman with the Blackened Shells of 86 Tortoises	47

Four

The Raccoon	57
Every Second	58
The Bay, Shimmering the Whole Way Out	60
Aren't We Lucky to Have Been So Beautiful	61
Tulips	62
Maybe the Wind Will Dance with Me	64
Great Meadows	66
Thinking About the Octopus	67
Looking for the Neowise Comet at Indian Neck Beach	68
Calling in the Grosbeak	69
Gas	70
Telescope on Brooklyn Sidewalk	72
And I Say Yes to the Way the Grass	73

Five

Little Prayer	77
Notes from the Column of Memory: Two	78
Galapagos Tortoise	80
Two Carp	81
Blue-Speckled Egg	82
Considering Cotton Candy	84
On the A Train, Manhattan	85
Visiting Your Graves in Denver	86
For My BRCA Gene Mutation	88
On Long Pond	91
Questions to the Screech Owl	92
This Fierce Elation	94
All the Hours the Night Has Left	96
Acknowledgments	99
About the Author	105

*I hope you love birds too. It is economical.
It saves going to heaven.*

—*Emily Dickinson*

*It is when you are asking about something that you realize
you have survived it, and so you must carry it,
or fashion it into a thing that carries itself.*

—*Anne Carson*

One

Red-Eared Slider

My baby turtle came from Woolworth's in a plastic tub,
a ramp running up the middle, a palm tree, also plastic,
and fishy-smelling flakes I'd pour into the water,
which got smelly, sickly sweet and sour, like a wet
swimming suit forgotten and left in a bag.

Once a week I put my turtle in a bowl to change the water.
I heard its little claws scraping the side, trying to get out. Once
I filled our bathtub with water and put my slider in to see
if it could swim. It could. Once I took it outside. I felt
sorry for it cooped up in that boring tub with only a fake
palm tree to play with. Which it didn't. Dumb palm tree.

I set my turtle gently on the grass and watched how hard
it had to work to crawl past blades of grass. When it strained
and stretched its neck way out, some streaky lines cropped up
that made me twinge. My turtle was so small in the grass.

Then I looked away to watch a cloud-shaped giraffe chew up
the cloud. When I turned back, my turtle was gone. I crawled
in circles on hands and knees, poking all around.

How could I have lost it? Or had I meant to free it, to give it
a better life? I worried what would happen when the mower
guy came the next day. I'd never even given it a name.

Corral

Somewhere my father had another
whole family I didn't know,
a wife I didn't know,

hardly ever saw. One son and a younger son.
Somewhere he lived with all of them
in a house. I went to that house once.

Was it brick, maybe, a lawn, some trees
living happily ever after.
I lived with my mother.

My father came for me on weekends.
Once he told me a secret about this family:
One of his sons wasn't his real son.

He told me no one else knew.
Perhaps he told me this to make me feel
special, because I was his favorite child,

his only daughter.
I liked keeping his secret,
he'd trusted me with it.

I guarded it desperately.
It charged around inside me
like a herd of horses galloping

across a vast bare plain.
To keep the horses safe, every time
I saw my father, I wore

the red cowgirl boots
he'd bought for me and made
of myself a corral.

My Father as a Taxidermied Fox

I've failed to flush an ounce of you from death.

Your boundary musk, your lunge and sprung plunge—
       refuse me.

You stalked nightly, your lair, some long-gone bramble,
             the kits you carried by the nape,

                 the shadow beneath your paw.
        Your secrets—the moles and voles and mice—

bristle the wire of your tail, stipple
             the fur on your flanks, crosshatch.

I do not dare, my hand that tries to trace
                your negative space.

How close you dared.

Fox who wandered into the barn, sniffed the cup
       of coffee on the floor.

You've stood on dunes and listened to foxes
        howl from the swale. And held your breath.

Groundhog

She scuttled out, shuddered, writhed in spasms
like a fish jerking on a line. I clutched
the wheel of the car, afraid to get out.

Then she threw herself on her back,
collapsed in small twitches on the sidewalk.

My god, how like sex it was. To be taken
so far out of your body you think
you're never coming back.

Then it was over. *You were never coming back.*

I got out and stared at her six swollen teats,
the soft belly fur, blonde as a wheat field,
the forepaws suspended and slightly rounded

as if in prayer, the short snout widening
to the lost pilots of the eyes, clockwork bite
of her incisors. And then a dark-gold stream

of urine spurted from her body like a dam
breaking open a lifetime of devotions—
muscles lined with coffers of winter fat,

sunlight, asters, and grass,
and the same sweet clover that stippled
the grass in my old backyard.

Oranges

Every morning my mother would pick
                      three soap-scrubbed oranges
    from the fridge's bottom bin,

                      slice them
and with the good palm
                      of her right hand she'd press
    each cut half

hard against the juicer's rotating drum,
        until everything that orange had been
                sluiced down

            into the round basin—nothing
left but the rind. Then she'd tilt
                      the juicer to catch

        the slow-moving rivulet of pulp and seeds
            against the strainer's

        teeth until only filtered juice
    drizzled into my glass and sparked orange-gold.

The all-at-onceness spilled on my tongue,
                the hustle of tart and sweet
        so sharp it hurt.

When my mother died—that burning
            bore through me, as if I had to

    do something about it. Or for it.
            Something I couldn't squeeze out.

Barbra Streisand Takes Her Two Cloned Dogs to Visit Their Mother

In the Instagram photo on her website, Miss Violet
(in lavender bandana), Miss Scarlett (in red),

on hind legs, their heads turned, peer over the top
of their stroller. Streisand writes, *My little girls were*

looking at their mother pictured on her gravestone.
Mother's face: a carved roundel on the granite slab.

The dogs are small, white and fluffy, a breed
I've never heard of, *Coton de Tulear.* Just before

their mother died, a doctor scraped cells from her
mouth and stomach. For $50,000 and change,

I could have done that, brought back my dog, Fella,
that black mutt. My mother named him after

FDR's dog Fala. I really miss my mother, too,
never got the chance to tell her I loved her.

Come to think of it, I miss my child self, troubled
as I was; my teenage years, riddled with insecurities;

my young-married self, full of Earth-Day hope;
my harried young-mother self. I miss my two children

when they were infants and I was sleep-deprived
and pricked my thumbs on diaper pins.

I miss my mother most of all. If I could have cloned her
before she died, I might have raised her as my own.

Hurled in the Grip

I'd asked the oncologist to call me if you were dying.
We're hopeful, he'd say. That's how he talked.

If I despaired, I was letting you down.
If I felt hopeful, I was deluding myself.

I was hurled in the grip. Rip-
tide pulling me out.

Thanksgiving, my stepfather hired a cook. We ate
at your table. Aunt, uncle, cousins.

You were stuck in the hospital,
I, too numb and under the thumb

of something huge, unspeakable.
Fear running through the gravy.

Aunt Norma told me she'd try to be a mother to me now.
She ate only a baked potato she mashed with her fork.

At your funeral, when I should have been rending
my clothes, I put on make-up, flirted with my old boyfriend.

I was 26. A body must break. My belly swelled up
just like yours, Mother. Terrified, I studied

the veins of my hands, the red and blue rivers
ready to burst. An electric fence circled my brain.

When I touch it in my Mother-dream,
I bolt awake.

Hurling the Menhaden

>   —*Herring Cove Beach, Provincetown*

This isn't a dream—blues have driven them in
        by the thousands, a broken silver chain I can't
              see the end of. Their gills
    are gashes, opening, closing on bare air.
Some are dead, or nearly.
            Some still squirming.
      I scoop one up, cup it slimy in my fist,
               hurl it back past the shallows
into deeper water. Hurl another
        to stay the extinction
      of the right whale. Another for
          my mother and another
for always running late. And the next for Yemen.
               And the next for never
     visiting my stepfather in the nursing home.
I throw them back faster and faster
        against the coming dark—

Bluebird

Blue as sapphires. As Monet's blue
water lilies. Put-down-your-burdens blue.
Stay-here blue and blue clear through. Lapis blue
of the Virgin's robe, the deep sea's untrammeled blue.
Blue as my valley, my shelter, my twilight mist, my thou-shalt-
not-want. Blue perches on the garden fence, sun catches the bright bead
of its eye. Blue swoops down to the sea of lavender bee balm,
crown vetch, black-eyed Susans. Bustling bees, bundled
in yellow sweaters, dip
their tongues into
the fringed petals
that sway with
the weight of the bees'
own bodies. I'd forgotten
beauty, its take-your-breath away, its
unexpected grace. How I'm helpless before it.
After days and days keeping the outside out, the inside in,
my heart retracted like a snail. *So haggard at the heart, so care-coiled,*
as Hopkins calls it. Come, sweet scent of mown grass, come, nectar
of my own sweet sweat. Come bluebird, flying now,
flown—carrying sky on your back.

Yellow Jacket

—after Vermeer's *A Lady Writing*

Years later, I read that the yellow jacket
she wore belonged to Vermeer,

only a prop, likewise, the string of pearls
she fingered on the table; that the fur trim

of her jacket was faux ermine (likely cat),
an opulent trick of the brush; her earrings,

glass beads, varnished like pearls. If this was
deceit, no matter. She wore all of it

the way purple martins wear barn light—
rivulets of lead yellow down her arm,

down the shaft of her quill, pressed to the page.
And on the wall behind her, *vanitas*—

the skull, the cello—cloaked with centuries.
She turned her face toward me, glancing up.

A smile in her eyes, which were looking
through me. We were already ghost.

Notes from the Column of Memory: One

See how time breaks us
and still we stand
among the flutings,
bearing traces
of triumph and ruin:
here are extinct
sea creatures,
their splattered blues,
lacy reds that hold
the lava of the living,
yellows flecked
with sun showers
from the dawn
of the cosmos, green
splashes of moss
from a colony
of hope. Peer into
the mirrored labyrinth
and you will see
your own face, fractured
but reclaimed, called back
to your history and your home.

Two

Outbreak

Some saw a raven with ruptured feathers.
Some smelled the homeless millions pressed
inside a drop of blood. Some felt dark planets
tilting. One planet, covered in octopi,
their arms entwined with acid from a toxic lockbox.
Another with the ghosts of dead tree frogs dancing
on shagbark. Some heard the dreams of the unborn
clinking cracked glasses. Some wept, clawing
the horizon. No Vacancy signs were visible
only in ice. Some thought they heard a saw blade
snap, but others insisted it was only a man
strangling on solar wind. Some swore they could
hear him rasp, throat choked on buckshot,
chanting a cantus firmus of forget-me-nots.

Traffic Jam on the 405 North

Estimated time in traffic is 15 minutes, the GPS says,
and what a mess we've made of us, five lanes wide,
the mass and rush of us, smog on the horizon,
and the billboard inviting us to exit at Manhattan Beach:
CNN Money's Best Place for the Rich and Single.

Hey, you in the KIA, you in the Jaguar, you
in the pickup truck in front of me,
your ladder strapped to sacks of insulation.
Two or more of every you in every whizzing
car in the carpool lane, and you and I
in our rented Impala. You *are a little soul*

carrying a corpse, Marcus Aurelius says
that Epictetus said. *Little soul* LAX, *little soul*
listens to Bach, *little soul* sponges up the minutes
inside the steel boxes where each little soul is

bantamweight, boxing the timeline. Each little soul
is brine, frightened and hustling. Oh, people,
sheathe each vanishing second in daisies.

The Only Softshell Turtle in Walden Pond

I'm afraid for her as she begins
to scrape with her back legs—
and because her foot-wide shell
looks soft as a floppy felt hat.

She shuffles back into water, pokes
her head up like a snorkel, hauls herself
onto the beach. She's breathing
hard now, refusing to give up.

Her legs tear at the hard-packed sand,
which begins to yield
to her stubborn necessity.

The ranger has put up a hazard cone
and yellow tape to keep us back.

Her eggs, unfertilized, will never hatch.
But she buries them anyway—
born to this, bound to this.

Apology to My Ovaries

They plucked you out before you could kill me.
I had to make a clean sweep. Forgive me,

conductor of my train to the future—
my artist daughter of long fingers

and kindness, my son with his kilowatt wit
and quiver of dreams. You were my gardener,

my stockpot, my pantry, your shelves
filled with my lifetime supply.

My arbor, predesigned, assigned at birth.
My divine egg timer, my clock that never

needed winding. You were my pinkish-gray,
almond-shaped, and my God, you were brave,

wore menstruation like a brightly flowered dress.
And the bloody labor of your fields.

Your timely hatchery, your drop-down
deliveries, your tubes swaying like anemones.

I, too, thought we could wither together
into gentle senescence. Forgive me

for evicting you in your dotage, not even
a hearing, your desk cleared in an hour,

everything you'd ever carried weighing
just over two ounces. Forgive me,

you who were my wheelhouse, my work
horse, my backfill, my unpaid laborer.

You, who toiled decades deep in the mine of me.

To Prove That I Am Not a Robot

I check off three mountains.

I check off three crosswalks painted gold.

I check off fourteen images of tsunami waves.

I check off all eleven federal holidays
in reverse calendar order.

I check off five glaciers that are receding,
in order of their diminishment.

I check off the habitat corridors
of the Australian alpine grasshopper,
the glossy black cockatoo,
the long-footed portoroo.

I check off twenty-five states
with new voting
restrictions.

I check off the last known addresses
of six million unfixed
lead service lines.

I check off fifty-seven pairs
of socks of children
who have been
separated

from their parents
to prove that I am human.

Five Knots and a Space

A space to keep myself
    from forgetting
the lemon light of morning.

      A knot for the horse I rode bareback
    when I was ten. His chestnut coat gleaming
        with sweat in the sun. His tail
          streaming behind.
          Then the wind.

    A knot to hold the places
        I've lost—
    my hometown, my bike,
      my roller skates
    crisscrossing from here
to the longing folded inside.

A knot for my son
and my daughter.
  Never untied.

        A knot for you
    from the base of your throat
        to the split willows
    of your hands. Your laughter,
      my river of stars.

A knot for the lust of long ago,
   and the new lust that rises
   from the ashes. Not the fire.

The memory of the fire, and how
   it burned through us.

Eye of the Storm

All the days you dithered, staring into the corona
of a dahlia, trying to remember
which was the stigma and which the pistil.

And you still don't know. It's ok.
All the days you were too shy to ask.
When you were too hard on yourself.

All those years. When you cursed, when you
blamed your mother, when you went to bed
grumpy and should have talked it through.

Trying to do your best, trying to come
to the height of your powers until the very end,
the way my high school boyfriend

who became a photographer
and is dead now told me that to capture
the storm you had to be the eye.

Or my mother, loading the dishes
in the dishwasher, making *ikebana*
of them until she could no longer stand.

Why is it, the closer we get to the end,
pain everywhere, we're pummeling
at greatness, or goodness, or just trying

to beat the deadline? Can you blame the heart,
the poor heart, which didn't mean to save
the best for last? And often fails at that.

Géricault finished his last painting, of his own
left hand, eight hours before he died, at 33.
He must have pressed that hand down hard,

to seal it to the page, traced it in pencil,
then a wash of browns, ochre and olive
to make flesh faithful, loving the life of it—

the nails clean and quiet as nuns, the singular thumb—
and on cold-pressed paper he spread a sepia bed
for his hand to rest in its own shadow.

Cézanne Still Life Painted by My Mother

Here in my dining room, your painted copy
of Cézanne hangs over the dry sink you bought
with Father years before I was born.

Did you paint what you needed for yourself,
freeing your good hand, leaving the laundry
and roast beef to marry

the grain of the table, stiffen the white cloth
to creamy peaks? Was it with mischief or delight
or both you picked up your palette knife

to slather Cézanne's lemon with slabs
of chrome yellow? Lost in the emptiness
between jug and teapot? Perhaps you stopped

fretting about me for the sake of that shallot.
In the corner, a dribble of taupe from your brush.
I run my finger over the dried slope

to stroke myself back to you, then lift
the frame from the wall to search
for your signature. Nothing

but your ghost and incurable distance,
and at the center—light
dancing on the bell of the jug.

Winter Ghazal

See how the snow leaps and dances, gray-sparked in winter.
Is it to reassure us not everything grows dark in winter?

Love unties its knot, takes flight in any air or season.
Warblers leave before the broken dark of winter.

You broke my heart and couldn't say where love had fled.
Had it been starved, long underfed? Love disembarked in winter.

Snow falls free of any human misery.
One must have a mind of winter to bear the bark and bite of winter.

From the train, I see a tall oak, with branches bare—
Oh, to perch there, perceiving all, the sharp-eyed owl in winter.

Coming Upon a Young Screech Owl

Face down on the sidewalk, his head to one side.
I squatted, stroked his ear with two fingers—

not sleeping, then: a small wildness, frozen dead.
I ruffled the barred feathers of his neck,

which were as light as air, pleated brown and white.
Stared at the side of his face I could see—

flat as a dish—and the one eye, open, the iris
drained of yellow, the pupil dark-stunned

with unbecoming. I thought to pluck a feather,
then hated myself. I traced the softness down

to his legs: the talons deep in the neck
of a rabbit kit, smaller than my hand.

Was a rabbit too heavy for a young owl
to carry? The owl distracted by headlights?

As if knowing could save me. But never
mind. Owl and rabbit are equals now, the rabbit

tucked beneath the owl's feathered cape.
I'll soon forget about the rabbit. It's you, owl,

little urgent one, living and dying by your wits.
You haunt me: stubborn seizure, grip of talons

that refuse, even in death, to release
what is yours, by rights, to take.

At Intermission

   1
I stood to stretch before the second act
and saw my ex-husband seated
in front of me. I called out to him,
my voice strong, *Hi, Jeff.*
He turned, stared. *I'm sorry*, he said,
but have we met? I whispered,
You're kidding? It's me, Wendy.

Your hair looks so different, he said.
I wondered if I was to apologize, a joke,
then, about my hair, to relieve my shame,
or to relieve him of his? Was I to giggle,
do a little dance? The sobering
and irrefutable music of the wife
I'd been strumming through me.

   2
Years ago, the Romas of Bulgaria
kept dancing bears, pulled them
around by metal rings inserted
through their noses. The bears had to stand up
on their hind legs to dance for tourists.
They weren't allowed to hibernate.

When the bears were freed, years later,
to sanctuaries, they hibernated
for the first time that first winter.

Then they woke up and didn't know
what to do. They began to stand
on two legs. They began to rock
back and forth and side to side.
They began to dance.

The Gannets at Cape St. Mary's, Newfoundland

Barbara says there are fewer
                nesting pairs this year. I can't see

     the missing, only the sea stack
swarming with thousands of birds, a fever

            of birds, pairs nesting on narrow shelves,
racket of wind-whipped screeches and grunts,
      the air acrid with guano.

Walking back along the cliff, I bend down to finger
      a broken shell tangled in caribou moss,

         tuck the pieces in my pocket,
     throw them away that night.

You can't keep
     every broken thing.

          I thought maybe the rock walls
could last. Stones fall, clattering
     against themselves, the way the heart

        of an unborn chick
                  beats faster the first time
     it hears the family song,

precise lifeline of notes
    that chick must learn. I thought

            all birds sang for beauty.
            Not for beauty. I'll learn
        to love them more for that.

Three

Burial of a Woman with the Blackened Shells of 86 Tortoises

—*Southern Levant, 10,000 BCE*

*

What if 40 shells had been placed in her grave,
one for each of her years? I hope they held
a shelf for sorrow, eased her husband's grief
for her hair, her sighs, her voice. A ritual spell,
the leg of a boar on her shoulder to widen the way.
Could those pelts have kept her from the cold,
the two stone martens they spread across her body,
and liquefaction of her soul, that stole
that warmed her breasts? I hope she loved, and hard,
that the aurochs' tail steadied her spine.
and the eagle's wing was transport, carried her
past the uphill grass to outlast time.
Sprinkled like holy water, those tortoise shells,
with or without the need for heaven, for hell.

*

With or without the need for heaven, for hell,
I clutched my bony rabbit's foot for luck—
the rabbit dead, the foot chopped off. Cruel,
that crisp, gold-capped clasp. No blood. No muck.
At night in bed I stroked the silky fur,
brown and white, slept with the chain so tight
around my finger it left a faithful ring.
The lore: kill the rabbit in the night,
a graveyard moon, the rabbit set down, crying
like a natural child. And I'm stuck
on why they placed a hacked-off human foot
inside the woman's grave—was that for luck?
Must we kill, need we sever,
to turn ourselves golden and forever?

*

To turn ourselves golden and forever,
that's what we want, but I don't really know
what my mother wore for her burial,
her lavender Ultrasuede or did someone sew
a shroud? Was she sleeked in the full-length mink
my stepfather gave her? Did she crave a slub
of silk from her father's vest? Maybe she wanted
her easel, back brace, blue rubber brush to scrub
each orange with soap. Where were the lace-up Oxfords
she needed (her ankles, weak), where was our family
dog, or his leg bone, at least? And what did she say,
last visit in Maine, as she was vanishing
at 56? After brief remission.
I forget what she said (forgive me), I didn't listen.

*

I forget what you said (forgive me), I didn't listen
until now, your voice in your letters, 50 years ago,
it's clear that something sharp had come between us—
barbs, worry, wishes, and warnings and scolds.
Closing my eyes, I smell your geraniums, the ones
with leaves like tongues, their ruddy scent. Your knack
for tackling dandelions. You loved your hands
in dirt. To nurture growth meant pinching back
the blooms. All those years you circled my pool—
stay out of the deep end, stay out of the sun.
Too many be-sure-to's and shouldn'ts. The spills I'd left
on the counter. Unsure of myself and whatever I'd done.
How hard you were trying to love your daughter.
What trouble we had, what turbulent water.

*

What trouble we had, what turbulence,
you'd speak to me in code, in nuts and bolts—
how long to cook a roast, best to soak
an egg pan in cold water, don't burn the toast—
when what I needed was metaphor, to link the distant,
a bridge over churning water to carry me past
your house to Saturdays with my weekend father:
the drive-ins and car rides with him rushed by too fast.
Mother, remember we watched *The Sound of Music*,
the motherless children, their bright-eyed, breezy new start.
The fairy-tale gloss: they never did cross
the Alps. The truth's like water, can't tease it apart.
It was myself I hadn't found.
A girl can easily run aground.

*

A grasshopper phobia ran you aground
each time you saw one. Once in the car, you swerved
to the curb, undone. Had a schoolboy stuffed one
down your blouse when you were young, unnerved you?
I could have taught you to love them, to see their claws
as supple strength. Your shield, that thistle-green thorax.
Their mandibles as sturdy as your will
to live. Their antennae as your last chance.
The music of hearing them rub the pegs on their legs.
I was your bell, you rang me faint and feeble.
You were my church, you preached and preached and preached.
And you were the steeple. I tried to climb to the people
you thought I needed to know. When I lean down,
I hear your silence working its way through the ground.

*

I hear your silence working its way through the ground
when I remember how I wanted to hurt you—
I'm never going to have children—so sure of myself,
my urge to dismantle my need for you, to refuse
what I knew you wanted. If I stitched you a quilt—
one patch for shame, one for sorrow, one
for when I wasn't there when you were dying.
One for my denying. I was undone.
I know you loved me hard. The way a mouse
licks and licks her babies, you licked me late
and long. I nearly drowned inside your spell.
Those licks. To keep me at bay or from harm's way?
I've only these 98 lines to soften, to save.
What if I'd placed 56 shells in your grave?

Four

The Raccoon

—Provincetown, Massachusetts

I'm eating a falafel sandwich on the deck at The Canteen
when from twilight I glean the dim shape crawling
along the ridge of the roof next door. Couples bustle
at the bar. The man at the table next to me sees it, too.
Trash pandas, he says, pointing, nuzzling the shoulder
of his bare-armed lover, licking her skin,

erotic prickle I thought was past, and the raccoon,
even at that distance, his loping, hunched back,
his enterprise so distant from mine—or was it?—
nipped at the shadowland between what I knew
as fear and what I claimed as love.

Out on the bay, the water (which before this
had appeared lighter than the sky), was darker,
sharpening the white hulls of boats, until the boundary
between water and sky, if there had been one,
dissolved, and the two darknesses, water and sky,
drank of one another, leaving the burning
and burned-out stars still shivering.

Every Second

By the time I swim back to the beach, the incoming
  tide has covered the sand bank. Far out where the bank
    had been, a boy and girl are splashing, kicking, gliding

  on the thin skin of water. I don't know if they feel it,
how I see them—triumphant, like messengers
    of the gods, or young gods themselves, not yet

knowing their fate. It was the unbrokenness I wasn't
  expecting—sun flowering, a slow field of light
    slipping from sea, slathering the eel grass;

  the horizon, a wide what-if. A buoy, a fin,
a row of dead squid washed up like a pack of cigars.
    That tinny song broadcasting

from a patio loudspeaker is a prayer I inhale hot.
  How many times did I tiptoe into my mother's bedroom,
    click open her beige leather clutch,

  dig beneath her spearmint gum, tissues
blotted pink, to open her wallet, wade in, steal a sea green bill
    with the pyramid with the creepy eye,

which, my friend Kay told me, was the eye of God,
  who looked down on all of us and could see
my every wrong. I never returned that dollar bill.

    I wade farther out. A cormorant lifts, wings heavy as hips,
flaps low and away. A hermit crab trawls sandy bottom, shuttling food
        into her mouth with her claws, sucking in

whatever's in reach in the shallows—plankton, seaweed,
    dead things—her scavenged shell so lush with algae
        it might be a hillside, glistening and green.

The Bay, Shimmering the Whole Way Out

The hull of a sailboat, yellow as a mango.
The sky's unbreachable blue. And a man

is riding a brown horse right in the bay.
Bareback, the water lapping his thighs, leading

another horse beside him. Out and back
they lope, cutting a broad swath as if

plowing a field, or harvesting one,
like a foreign language heard as pure music.

But there: two horses, brown as loam,
mowing the measureless rows, and that yellow hull,

rocking. A fruit I couldn't pick, beside my love,
wrapped in his summer scent, sea tang and brine.

Aren't We Lucky to Have Been So Beautiful

Nobody knows any more what the wind said
to the stone, or the deer to the grass. Maybe

it's true there's no thought without language,
just ideas written by the stars. Maybe silence

is itself an idea. Maybe time is silence.
Maybe a cucumber is incarnate and immortal,
bearing seed and born of seed. Maybe I'll learn

to do better, want less. It's late afternoon,
I watch geese stroke the pond. The sun hurls

our two shadows fifty feet down the slope,
sunlight roars over the rooftops, deckles clouds.

When I walk into my love's shadow,
we become a camel we ride together. I was five
when I stood beside the lilac in the backyard,

buds humming into blue air, tingling
with the honey-heavy scent, as if

hundreds of unspent pennies jangled
in my pocket, *my* pocket, and I realized—
I was I. Now my astonishment could begin.

Tulips

This morning the two red ones by the driveway have flung
    themselves wide open like mouths or sex or wounds,
and the other two, red also, but streaked with yellow flames

that leap all the way up, have done the same.
    Indigo explodes from the center of each bloom, circled
by a yellow ring of fire: nothing set aside for later,

all deep faith, *take me, take me*. And the stamen,
    swollen with pollen, and the pistil with its three stigmas
like tiny helpless animals. How can a body be

so unafraid— the dappled, the fringed, the narrow-waisted,
    the lily-flowered, the triumphs, the long-throated, dipped
in rubies, the quench-my-thirsts, the red, true-love tulips,

the white I'm-sorry tulips, the Queen of the Night wrapped
    in velvet, those turbaned tunic tulips, those nursery-
in-the-nectary tulips, the whorled, chaste, scentless tulips,

the ones with breaking virus, which damages the bulb
    but sets petals ablaze, like the one the Dutch went mad for
in 1637, the Semper Augustus: thirty-seven people paid more

for one bulb than what a skilled craftsman could make in a year.
    By five, under cloudy skies, the tulips in my driveway
have clamped shut, furled like rolled carpets.

Darkness, I, too, protect myself from, closing up
   late afternoons, turning tender to myself, listening
to consonants click together inside my mouth.

Maybe the Wind Will Dance with Me

Stopped next to me at the light, a cement mixer—
red and green cab as bright as Christmas.

Airbrushed over the fuel tank, swooping white lines,
like hovering angels. And on the side of the cab,

edged in delicate blue cursive, as if under
the bright wing of heaven

> *Tresca Bros. Concrete*

My longing: for the world to be better than it is.

Inside the mixer, grit and gravel, churning profit and loss,
but isn't something to be said for the graceful strut,

the slow rolling over? On this day, anyway,
the grinding hurry and traffic and worry, something

to be said for the muscular, the proud carriage,
the swill and hardness of concrete, the spinning

drum of the world in all its fearlessness—the caterpillar
when it squeezes out of its own skin, when it cocoons

into chrysalis. And what isn't the work
of transformation? I'm undone by the humming

of what-could-be, speak silver sheened, in tongues.
Polish myself on stones.

Great Meadows

I've come for the red-winged blackbirds,
their *conk-la-rees* and crimson, for the muskrat

nosing the edge of the marsh, wet brownness
from tapered nose to water-shine tail,

and I'm here for the burst pods of milkweed,
for the fallen tree, its upturned roots beyond my reach,

for the lichen that burgeons emerald all along
the trunk's flank, for these woods chock-full

of downed branches, broken branches entwined
with bittersweet vines, for the pursed fist

of swamp cabbage bursting through muck
and decayed leaves. This hard and ceaseless work.

Thinking About the Octopus

—after the film *My Octopus Teacher*

I'm thinking about how she opens every one of her three hearts,
    and all the brain cells in her eight arms,

        how she coils into a ball inside a cloak of shells and stones,
    wraps herself in a shawl of kelp so the shark won't see her,

            regenerates the arm the shark tore off,
    in seconds clothes herself in lionfish, flounder, sea snake—

then jets away like a rocket to slip inside a crack no larger
    than her own eye. I'm trying to understand what made her

        uncoil one shy arm to touch the hand of the filmmaker
    who'd dived down to her den twenty-six days in a row

        in the kelp forest off the coast of South Africa.
    And when she spurts through the water, hurls her whole

improbable body onto his chest, entwines her arms around him,
    clinging, how can you not call that tenderness?

    Don't you too want to find a way back to what
        we once were with each other, millions of years ago—
that common grammar, that syntax of salt and stars?

Looking for the Neowise Comet at Indian Neck Beach

I count three fists down
        and zipper those stars
                into the Big Dipper.

I want to tell you I see it, that comet,
        that I can name that cold smattering
              so it's large enough
        to quench my thirst.

Which is huge for the out there.

            Maybe it's only
my shaky hands gripping the binoculars
        that set a star I see to sizzling
            like a live wire.

Shouldn't it be enough
        the sky's an all-night Broadway show,
            an endless proscenium,
                the Milky Way riding
        the black everlasting?

            Shout *Hineni* to the great silence—
the still unfinished stories
    hurled out
into peacocking galaxies,
        turned into constellations,
            given their starry names.

Calling in the Grosbeak

I stand right behind the guide
            as he calls in the rose-breasted grosbeak
by turning on a speaker
        clipped to his belt.

    He lures the bird with a recording
of the grosbeak's own song across the meadow—

    the real bird swoops in,
        furious with cause and claim,
            adrenal-pumped, ready to confront.

He circles the precincts of air, chinks
        warning at us
           from a nearby tree.

Angry, anxious. Tones and half-tones
    like a waterfall.

I've come here to infuse the sweetness,
           and now I've got him
        in my scope—the ivory beak,
    the scarlet breast
        like a wound.

Gas

It's 6:30 and the attendant at Nick's Service Station
in my town is closing up for the night, setting out bright
orange plastic traffic cones. He might be Nick and he might

also be the "Master Mechanic on Duty" as the sign
above the bay door says. He's leaning on his cane
as he moves one cone a few inches away from another,
getting the spacing exactly right. Now his hands linger

as he unkinks hoses on a pump, settling them down
for the night. And I'm thinking of Hopper's *Gas*,
the attendant behind the pump doing something we can't

see as he leans into the work in the dimming light. I lean, too,
soaked in the silence of dusk, in the lollipop-red of the three
pumps that glow like little moons. I orbit around and past them,
skirt the girth of hemlocks that are scooping up the darkness.

You don't want to go into those woods, either, do you?
So you fall down along the ribbon of red-tinged grasses,
traverse the strip of macadam that bends slightly right

and out of sight. No one's there for you. So you come back
to the path of white neon that streams from the station windows,
enfolds the pumps, and even though it's an empty, sharp
kind of light, it's all there is to hold on to. Let's cling to it,

Nick. Don't close the station now. Take my hand, we can stroll to the *Mobilgas* sign that towers over the tallest tree. Let's climb the pole, mount the red-winged horse threshing that sky-high field.

Telescope on Brooklyn Sidewalk

It was dusk, the street corner buzzing like a hive,
a telescope there on the sidewalk, its giant eye
tilted toward the moon. I stopped, marveling,
moved closer—a man gestured with his open palm,
have a look. I lowered my eye to the lens,
which was as private as a peephole, peered down
the tunnel, risqué and mine alone to enter.

I recoiled at the blast—there were craters close enough
to swallow me, and where the waxing crescent
curved away it was like walking into the valley
of the shadow of death, and the whiteness, stark
and scarred, was blinding, a comfortless cold,
all that light coming from the other side of the world
where the sun hadn't yet set.

That moon, I tell you, was dazzling and terrifying
and desolate—not one tree or garden or fountain,
no bees or tigers or bodegas selling milk or cracked
concrete cooling into the night, no cars or car radios
blasting, no mercury or corroded lead pipes or any
of the other things that are killing us or being killed
by us—my god, that moon filled my every pore
and I dove into silence.

And when I ripped away my eye, I was jolted
by the shudder of air around my shoulders,
so many people swirling by, swaddling me
in their din and swish and swell.

And I Say Yes to the Way the Grass

needs the soil, and the soil needs the grass,
the way the candle needs the wick and the wick,
the candle. Yes to the way the lion and the buck

need one another, and the bluebird the caterpillar.
To the ocean that needs a shore for its waves.
Yes to the cymbals for needing the violins,

and violins for needing the winds, to the four
winds and the sixteen quarter winds
and the thirty-two winds it takes to make

a compass rose. Yes to each petal that needs
the other forty petals to be a rose, and to the rose
for holding all the petals before letting them die

for the new bud. Yes to the stars, closing
their eyes at the same time to darkness,
yes to the rain in the valley of thirst.

And I say yes to the time we live with because
we've got to live with it, yes to loving better,
to coming in from anywhere.

Five

Little Prayer

—for Barbara Helfgott Hyett

The magnolias have opened
their milk-white stars for you
above the shatter.

Over granite and over
the smallest pebble,
may the streams run clear.

And where there was once hunger,
let the deer find berries and bark
in this unfamiliar grove

where you trace the outline
of your body on air
to fill the reservoir
of your brand-new name.

And when you find yourself lost
like an ant in the petals of the peony,
remember your life's work
has always been
to help the flower open.

Notes from the Column of Memory: Two

Sometimes you see a column
of stones and think
it's a mountain.
Sometimes what seems
like a mountain
is only a pile of stones.
Sometimes you see
the shadow of a bird
pinned to the sky
after the bird flies.
Sometimes the ground
blurs before your eyes
and you can no longer
see the horizon.
We are
so precarious.
Remember
when touching and being
touched plunged you
into the very quick of it—
your laughter crackling
inside your mouth,
your heart
a swinging door
opening and closing
and opening
to the fissure of years.
Listen and you can

almost hear waves
rippling through
flecks of feldspar,
the Milky Way balancing
the night sky.

Galapagos Tortoise

They slept together in shallow scrapes,
extended their necks to invite finches.
So tame. It took meat-starved men

to roll each tortoise over, lash the legs
to long poles, carry them back to the ship,
hundreds in a single day. Stacked

on their backs, they could live
for a year: no food, no water.
Fresh meat, roasted right in the shell.

The ones not eaten were sold on shore,
their plates boiled, flattened for knitting
needles, bangles, tea caddies, and the comb

my father gave my grandmother.
When she wore it in her hair,
the reddish-brown flames caught the light.

Two Carp

—after *Fish and Turtles* by Maruyama Ōkyo (1733–1795)

Sheathed in the pulse
        of sinew and nerve, they are precisely
                carp. Fleshy wet. Sweep and shimmy.

    Their scales like chain mail as they
shimmer and flex in the vastness
        of a tea ceremony screen.
    Beneath them, pale blue water ripples
on a second painted layer of silk,

their taut bodies suspended, as in a dream,
        as if they hesitate only because I am watching them.

        Haven't you, too, tried to hold a river
to your ear to hear the wild roar of what is?

Blue-Speckled Egg

Fog spreads
itself along
the unbuttonable
shore.

On the side
of a cliff,
caribou moss
as warning.

If I'm a gannet,
I'll fly
to your ledge.
You'll know me
by my crown.

If I'm the brimming
ravaged, I'll be fire,
quenched by
the coarse breath
of air.

If I'm regret
turned inside out,
keep me safe
from ravens.

Then sing me
the family song
I've never heard.

Considering Cotton Candy

Nothing but spun cloud and sugar. And that pinkness,
as pink as your mother's "Love That Pink" lipstick,
your pink poodle skirt, the showiest azalea.
As if a sugar plum princess had swirled her wand
into a whirl of windblown light and will-o'-the wisp.

Was it one time, or many, I pulled my father
toward the circus vendor, spellbound as he dipped
the wand of white paper, twirled his hand
round and round until the whirling frothed into being,
as sumptuous as Cinderella's gown—then handed it to me.

What child doesn't need a little magic?
That first bite, or slurp, or inhalation,
what can I call it? Pure bliss? Maybe
the second bite, too. The third? By then
my hands were sticky, my cheeks sugar smeared,
the perfect pillow of fluff teetering,
the whole confection threatening to tumble down.
The crunchy bits of grit sickeningly sweet,
the weightlessness turned to waste and what now.

And it was air I bit into, like everything
I couldn't keep, that wouldn't last
past midnight as I rode back with my father
to my mother's house. Was I the high-wire act,
was I the juggler, or was I one of his
spinning plates traded hand to hand, midair?

On the A Train, Manhattan

A man holding the pole with one hand, an iPhone with the other,
working a crossword's checkered semaphore of blacks and whites,
each space to be girded with meaning. He pecks one letter

at a time with his thumb. His fingers are stubby, like my father's.
The letters tumble into place, and the nails of his other hand,
the one holding the pole, are painted sea-foam green,

each finger's polished half-moon like a genie prancing—
until he lifts that hand and the nails belong to the woman
standing behind him— everyone entangled with illusion—

my father, eighteen years dead, is driving me back
to my mother's house. I'm eight, and we're doing *here is the church* . . .
here is the steeple . . . pressing my fingers into the spire,

open the doors . . . *all the people* springing from my own
two hands, squeezing through the subway's sliding doors,
until my father kisses me good-bye for the week, walks away.

Visiting Your Graves in Denver

FindAGrave.com has a glitch.
I circle the cemetery for an hour

until I find you, Mother. The only-ness of stone,
the loneliness of stone, the slab

on which your second husband wrote:
I will love her forever.

No *Daughter of,* *Mother of,* No *Sister of,*
whose grave lies next to yours.

My stepfather's grief honed that stone, hoarded love.
My grief, unrecorded, turned in and ate itself.

    *

Across town, among these pines,
the Drexler monument, your name's

sharp chisel. No one has come to place
a stone, not your new wife, not your sons.

I will. Can't find a pretty round one.
Tell myself a pebble will do. Didn't I do?

Wasn't I your *girl* who traded
weekday absence for your weekend

Corvette, the red cowgirl boots
you bought me, the roller coaster rides?

       *

    Mother. Father.
    My name is Wendy,
    daughter of Hannah,
    daughter of Stanley.

Yitgadal v'yitkadash sh'mei raba.

For My BRCA Gene Mutation

—I am obliged, now, to refrain from dying, for as long as it is possible.
—Lucie Brock-Broido

Recitative
All these years you've been lying
in wait, trying to kill me.

So I drive fast past the marsh
choked with loosestrife.

Obliged now, I lunge into icy ocean to sting myself
senseless. I stop to buy myself
a double-dip soft-serve at the drive-in

where the counter girl swirls a spiral
to the mound's flared tip.

Chocolate oozes down. I crunch
that cone to crumbs.

Where are my lance, my shield,
and my greaves?

Don't fondle me.
Don't beggar.
Don't guzzle my sunset.
Don't ladder my ribs.

Don't tribal, don't
Pied Piper my cells
            over a cliff.

Take my ovaries—they're nothing
to me now. Not my breasts, shape-shifter.

And keep your goddamned devil's hands
off my daughter, my granddaughter,
the present continuous.

Let me beat another little riff
with her on her toy drum.

   Aria
You zipped into me right from the zygote,
looping through my bloodline. Do you know we go

back and back? That after you left Budapest to nest
in my grandmother's breast, you glided inside

my mother's pancreas, my Aunt Norma's pancreas?
I know I've bad-mouthed you, but this time

I'll go out of my way not to step on your toes.
Yes, the toes are our little joke. Listen: Why kill me off

when we can watch mourning doves balance
on the telephone wire, laugh at the weightlessness

of dandelion seeds riding the wind, and sing
to a passing cloud—can you believe something

that looks so light weighs a million pounds!
I keep looking out for you, little sequence,

little squeeze-box, little bracelet wrapped round
my every cell. Little carrier, little launchpad,

little keepsake, I'm bracing for your broken pin stripe,
your falter in the halter of me, your faultline

on my chromosome 17. Why in service to you
just last Sunday I wore a mask to the hospital—

lay down inside the metal womb to illuminate
any nuggets you might've left in my breasts.

For you I let the magnets rap and rattle
and knock through me. Thank you for

not this time. Oh, little ripcord on my parachute,
I know we've tied the knot. A lifetime. A lifeline.

You're immortal. I know
where I'm bound. No hard landings, please.

Let's float gently, together, all the way down.

On Long Pond

Morning fog   a blur of firs   light-green on the far shore
    I look up   a flock of swallows unfurls
        over the pond   stitching the air   with swift flickering

        a few birds turn   more turn   a loose confederacy
        that keeps the flock together   my mind swooping
to that far-from-here backyard   the lilac's honey

my mother dragging the hose   deadheading geraniums
    me in the sandbox   digging tunnels   to China
        go, go, go   says the bird

    the fog deepens   into a flock   of silence
        that echoes   long after   the bell has been rung

Questions to the Screech Owl

—*after W. S. Merwin*

do you notice   our telescopes set up across the street
do you mind us watching you & how large we are
what do you think   of the wild turkeys that roost in the tree behind you
do you like birds   are the crows too noisy
how deep is that cavity   have you lined it with something soft
do you sleep soundly all day   did the roofers disturb you last week

where are you   when you are not here
do you prefer bones or meat   which is more sweet salty savory
do you take your meal   in a single gulp or long slow bites
do you hunt every night   do you wake up hungry
how hungry is hungry for you   do you hunt on the wing
do you wait for the right color   the right silence to leave every night at dusk

who was with you   in the cavity last spring
why did she leave   did you fight or just not get along
will you look   for another
have you ever had young   did they all fledge

do you remember your mother or father   did they sing you to sleep
what do you love   most about the darkness
how it folds around you   or how it cuts through you like satin
are these the same thing to you   are you ever cold & do your bones ache
are you ever lonely   can you hear yourself think
what frightens you most   about the sky
are you ever claustrophobic   have you ever been lost

what did you see last night   do you ever feel rushed
do you ever get bored   what do you do when you don't feel well
do you dream   when you first wake up
do you know where you are   & who you are
do you have nightmares   how do you get back to sleep
which is your favorite   wind moaning in the branches
the bark breathing   snow falling
your wings skimming the air   the light sifting
susurra of rain   the crunch of a rabbit kit's bones in your mouth
what frightens you just a little   can you sleep through thunder
do you prefer the thin light of winter   to the thickness of summer
do you know what kind of tree this is   do you know that it's dead
do you have questions   for the moon

This Fierce Elation

    —after the photo *Autumn Abundance* by Yvette Melzer

Look into this window with me:
all these tomatoes ripening
on the sill, their fleshy heft caressed
by light—these Romas in a bowl
are fire-engine red and then a chime
of tangerine, then Brandywine,
then one creamy white that rests
upon the shoulders
of a large-lobed Heirloom,
a peek of tiger—as if their flesh
will never be blemished or blighted,
always this empire of ruby,
amber, sandstone, the promise
of salt on the counter, the knife's
slice, and seduced as I am
by such fierce elation, I haven't
noticed until now there's a woman
behind them, camouflaged
against the sepia background
(her kitchen?), thin-strapped chemise,
bare shoulders, a mug of coffee
in her hand, and now I look harder,
the woman's fingers are clenching
the handle of the mug, her grip insisting
I see the work of holding on—
planting the seeds in soil, watering,
weeding so the seeds would cling

to earth, staking the sprouting tendrils,
holding each ripe tomato in her
cupped palm, confirming wholeness,
before she picked them one by one,
placed them gently in her basket
and carried them into her kitchen,
setting them down on that sill—
I see you, vigorous parade
of tomatoes, woman with your still-
warm cup of coffee in your hand.

All the Hours the Night Has Left

What I'll never have is close to, or nearly equals,
what I've had. I find myself at equilibrium,

which may last only a day—the mayfly's
brief happiness—no way of knowing

if this is happiness or merely the acknowledgment
of where I am, skittering and buzzing and looking

all around, the pond by now thick with my own kind,
the water the halfway shade of tea light and twig—

it no longer matters I can't see clear
like the elephant god, remover of obstacles.

The first time I heard a concerto, and someone
told me what makes a key minor

is the lowered third, I listened to the sorrow
for myself. At last I can name it:

brokenness, beauty, the way through.

Acknowledgments

I am grateful to the following publications in which these poems first appeared, some under different titles, others in different forms:

Art on the Trails: Mending: "Notes from the Column of Memory: One"

The Atlanta Review: "Telescope on Brooklyn Sidewalk"

Barrow Street: "At Intermission," "Barbra Streisand Takes Her Two Cloned Dogs to Visit Their Mother," "For My BRCA Gene Mutation: Aria"

Cider Press Review: "Traffic Jam on the 405 North"

The Comstock Review: "My Father as a Taxidermied Fox," "Yellow Jacket"

Emergence: Plein Air Poetry: "Bluebird"

Hare's Paw Review: "On Long Pond"

Ibbetson Street: "Hurled in the Grip," "Visiting Your Graves in Denver"

The Lily Poetry Review: "The Gannets at Cape St. Mary's, Newfoundland," "Great Meadows," "Little Prayer," "Winter Ghazal"

Mom Egg Review: "For My BRCA Gene Mutation: Recitative"

Muddy River Review: "The Only Softshell Turtle in Walden Pond"

Nimrod: "The Bay, Shimmering the Whole Way Out"

One Art: A Journal of Poetry: "All the Hours the Night Has Left"

Pangyrus: "Outbreak"

Prairie Schooner: "Corral"

RHINO: "Galapagos Tortoise"

Rockvale Review: "Every Second"

Salamander: "On the A Train, Manhattan"

Solstice: "And I Say Yes to the Way the Grass"

South Florida Poetry Journal: "Thinking About the Octopus"

Sugar House Review: "To Prove That I'm Not a Robot"

SWWIM: "Apology to My Ovaries"

Tar River Poetry: "Aren't We Lucky to Have Been So Beautiful"

The Threepenny Review: "Coming Upon a Young Screech Owl"

Twelve Mile Review: "Burial of a Woman with the Blackened Shells of 86 Tortoises"

"And I Say Yes to the Way the Grass" was also published on masspoetry.org for Mass Poetry's online series, *The Hard Work of Hope*, and was featured on a placard in the window of the Harvard Coop, Cambridge, Massachusetts, as part of the Harvard Square Poetry Stroll, December 11, 2021 – January 2, 2022.

"Burial of a Woman with the Blackened Shells of 86 Tortoises" was featured on *Verse Daily*, March 26, 2022.

"This Fierce Elation" was featured on *Autumn Sky Poetry Daily*, May 9, 2022.

"Notes from the Column of Memory: One" received the Juror's Prize for the winning poem and was published in *Art on the Trails: Mending* (eds. Cynthia Franca, Maura Snell, and Catherine Weber). The poem was inspired by Donna Conklin King's sculpture of the same name, which was part of an installation at the Beals Preserve, Southborough, Massachusetts, summer 2021.

My deep thanks to my family and friends for their love and support, and to my poet friends Cynthia Bargar, Nancy Esposito, Vivian Eyre, Eric E. Hyett, and Fred Marchant for their close reading, early or late, of this manuscript, and for their essential feedback. The poets in my weekly workshop have individually and collectively kept me going, especially over the last two years during which we have met online: Cynthia Bargar, Vivian Eyre, Xiaoly Li, Steve Nickman, Sarah Dickenson Snyder, Connemara Wadsworth, and Margot Wizansky. Thanks to the community of friends and poets in my free write group, who heard many of these poems take their first breath, including Steve Ablon, Alexis Ivy, and Susan Pizzolato; to my poet sisters from the Fine Arts Work Center, including Jane Bachner, Anna Birch, Lin Illingworth, Phyllis Katz, Myrna Patterson, and Marilyn Potter; to my teachers at the Fine Arts Work Center over several summers, for their inspiration: Gabrielle Calvocoressi, Martha Collins, Nick Flynn, Marie Howe, and Carl Phillips, and to the poets who shared that workspace; and to Luci Huhn. My gratitude for the affirmation and financial support of the Massachusetts Cultural Council for awarding me a 2022 artist fellowship. With abiding love to my longtime mentor and dear friend, Barbara Helfgott Hyett, who knew how to lead a poem to water *and* teach it to drink, and who has taught me so much of what I know about writing with craft and with courage. Deep gratitude to my children, Noah Baron and Julia Price Baron, for their inspiration, love, and assistance in all things; and to my husband, Herb Friedman, for his abiding love and support.

About the Author

Wendy Drexler is the recipient of a 2022 artist fellowship from the Massachusetts Cultural Council. She is the author of two earlier collections, most recently, *Before There Was Before* (Iris Press, 2017). Her poems have appeared in *Barrow Street, Nimrod, Prairie Schooner, The Threepenny Review,* and *Valparaiso Poetry Review,* among others. Her work has been featured on *Verse Daily* and WBUR, and in numerous anthologies. She has been the Poet-in-Residence at New Mission High School in Hyde Park, Massachusetts, since 2018, and is programming co-chair for the New England Poetry Club. She lives in Belmont, Massachusetts.

www.wendydrexlerpoetry.com

www.ingramcontent.com/pod-product-compliance
Lightning Source LLC
Chambersburg PA
CBHW030156100526
44592CB00009B/310